This book is dedicated to the memory of my mother

DeRosette Clarinda Willie Horne Casey
whose voice of encouragement was always
whispering in my ears and still she speaks to my heart.

Jackson County, Western North Carolina

A PICTORIAL HISTORY

The African Americans Of Jackson County

From Slavery to Integration

by Victoria A. Casey McDonald

*Published with funds provided in part by a Grassroots Arts Program Grant
from the North Carolina Arts Council
and the Jackson County Arts Council
With assistance from the North Carolina Community Foundation*

Catch the Spirit of Appalachia, Inc.
Western North Carolina

FIRST EDITION 2006

Layout/Edited by Amy Ammons Garza
Cover Illustration by Doreyl Ammons Cain

Publisher:

Catch the Spirit of Appalachia, Inc.

Imprint of Ammons Communications — SAN NO. 8 5 1 – 0 8 8 1
29 Regal Avenue • Sylva, North Carolina 28779
Phone/fax: (828) 631-4587

Library of Congress Control Number: 2006933576
ISBN 10: 0-9753023-6-1
ISBN 13: 978-0-9753023-6-1

*Note: The information contained in this book is not necessarily in chronological order.
Every attempt was made to correctly identify each person. Photos are from family collections
unless otherwise noted. Photos of less quality (aged/faded) have been inserted because of the
significance of the era and human history.*

Dreams are like flashes of lightning that brighten up the night on a warm summer afternoon. They are there just for a moment, and then disappear into the atmophere. The aftermass engulfs us. . .as thunder roars across the heavens, letting us know that dreams have a life.

In 1981, thunder exploded for me as Dr. Clifford R. Lovin, a friend and history professor at Western Carolina University gave me the opportunity to begin my dream of researching the African American History of Jackson County, North Carolina. Cliff told me about the North Carolina Humanities Committee who were awarding mini-grants to individuals to do research that could be presented to the adult population of the area. He gave me the form for the grant. I filled it out and sent it to them.

Weeks later, the rain poured when I was awarded $1000 dollars to do research on the black history of the county. It was the spring of 1981.

Through the sponsorship of the Black Community Development Club of Jackson County, which was under the auspices of Mountain Projects, I was given the task of presenting a slide-tape show on the African American population of the area. I focused my show on the African American social, political, religious and economic contributions. My research spanned more than hundred years—from 1865 to 1967. The title of the slide-talk show was *"Looking Back Before Integration."* This slide show has made its rounds in Western North Carolina and parts of it were presented at the Appalachian Conference in Blacksburg, Virginia.

During the two decades following, I have completed a text to accompany the photographs gathered from my research, some of which is presented in this book. The photographs shared with you here were not taken by me, but by amateur African Americans and/or white professional photographers. I chose these pictures to present the history of black Jackson County through the years of segregation. I am continually gathering other photos that can depict the coming age of the African American in the county.

My dream has become a bolt of lightning illiminating the sky and has taken a life of its own. Now let it thunder.

—*Victoria A. Casey McDonald*

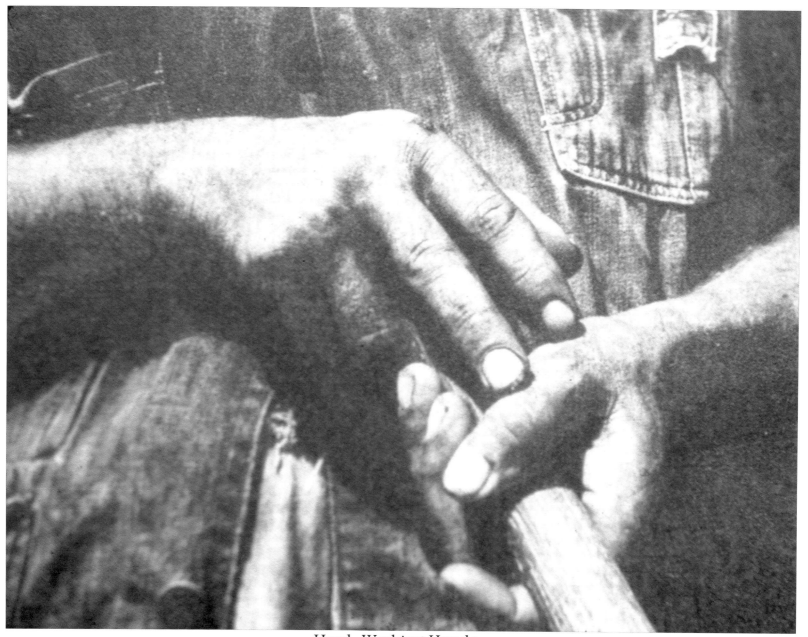

Hard, Working Hands

6

Table of Contents

Sadie Hooper Casey, the grandmother of author, photographed in early 1900's.

This is a pictorial history of African Americans in Jackson County, North Carolina. It will show historical pictures from about 1890 until 1965 when the African American school closed its door. Many images have been lost and not recorded. Before the Civil War, a large number of African Americans were slaves in this mountainous terrain of North Carolina. After emancipation the relationship between master and slave continued without the force of the law. With the expansion of the county's economic base, African Americans and whites worked side by side.

After Reconstruction the revision made in the state constitution made it virtually impossible for African Americans to vote or hold public office. In Jackson County, segregation brought isolation to the scattered African American communities. However, they created their social and political structure by establishing their own churches and schools. This allowed the African Americans to nurture their own identity and self-worth. These two institutions cemented the small black communities together.

Viewing the photographs in this book, one will see that the more important of these two institutions was the school. The consolidation of the schools allowed the scattered black communities to become one. The African American community in Jackson County, along with Swain and Macon counties, were educated by going from a one-room structure in each isolated community to a plank two-winged building with a gym in the center, to a brick building with central heating and inside plumbing, When the consolidation occurred, the African American students were assembled under one roof. About 75% of the teachers were from Jackson County and some teachers were second and third generation.

Following the Civil War, African Americans remained with the white churches they had attended as slaves. In the 1870's customs began to change. The freed men asked their former masters to allow them to establish their own church. Permission was granted and churches began to organize in each community. Most of these communities established a Baptist church, as well as a Methodist church. The majority of the preachers were itinerant. The churches together, although different denominations, established a joint fifth Sunday meeting during the 1930's through 1960's. It was called the *Feast in the Wilderness,* bringing together the Methodists and the Baptists. Sometimes it was difficult to know who was Methodist and who was Baptist.

Hence, the functions of African American

churches and the school intertwined. The church addressed the African Americans' spiritual, political and social issues, while the school attended to issues of education. Hand in hand they wove a solid foundation, that was eventually torn asunder by integrating into the various community white schools.

Amanda Thomas Casey was the slave of William Holland Thomas, the white Chief of the Cherokee. Her mother, Martha, was thought to be the first slave of Thomas. Amanda died in 1924. The author of this book is Amanda's great granddaughter.

When the Civil War ended, the problems of the newly freed African Americans were multiplied. In Jackson County the small population of African Americans wanted to become citizens. With the hope of being accepted as equal, legalizing their marriages with the state of North Carolina was perhaps the first step in becoming a part of the Southern society. African Americans began to find their own way. Farming was perhaps the only occupation most of them knew; therefore they began by purchasing a piece of land and went about making a living for their families.

The county had an influx of former slaves from the bordering states of Georgia and South Carolina.There were 33 black farmers and 66 black farm laborers listed in the county's 1865 census.The black population was 266 as the 1870 year began. By 1880 the black population had tripled and continued to grow in the decades before the 20th century.

Former slave Lou Bryson received her

This picture represents the influx of African Americans into Jackson County after the Civil War as they moved from bordering states of Georgia and South Carolina to find acres of land to farm.

11

acreage of mountainous terrain in the River View section of Dillsboro from her former master, Thaddeus D. Bryson. Others like Silas Davis bought their land. On May 24, 1872 George Rogers bought a hundred-acre tract of land from W. P. Woods for $450. Bill and Amanda Casey purchased land in the Cullowhee area from M. L. Dietz for $300. Most of the land the former slaves purchased was in large quantities, but much of it was not suited for farming.

In the decades that followed, the African Americans found other ways to support their families. In 1868 a mica mining company in the area of Webster hired both black and white workers.

These men are black and white miners from the Cullowhee area, who worked in the mica mine at Long Branch.

12

By 1900 the value of mica production in the county was $7000 dollars and rose to $8,740 dollars the next year. Colonel C. J. Harris built an industrial empire in the county. He, too, hired both black and white workers in mining and tanning industries in Sylva and Dillsboro.

Other economic opportunities were also presented to the newly freed slaves. Robert Lee Madison established the Cullowhee Normal School (Western Carolina University) and blacks were able to obtain employment there. Hotels around the area of Webster, Dillsboro and Sylva gave jobs to blacks.

The Western Carolina Railroad was still under construction, and according to the 1870 census of Jackson County, seven African Americans were employed as railroad laborers. These workers were James Casey, John Baggleton, Solomon, John Horton, Bayles Harriston, Gelbert Christan and John Boyles. All had emigrated to Webster from Tennessee except Casey, who was born in North Carolina.

These unknown men are railroad laborers working for the Western Carolina Railroad.

With the ability to earn a living for their family, the African Americans sought to stabilize

their lives in other areas. As slaves the African Americans were introduced to Christianity and the church. It was important that Sunday was set aside for worship. Therefore, they continued to worship with their former owners. It was not unheard of that blacks and whites worshiped together before the Civil War. In 1853, there were eight "colored" members of the white Webster Baptist Church.

It has been traditionally stated that the black Webster Baptist Church was the first African American church in the county. However, in May of 1871, former slaves who were members of Scotts Creek Baptist Church asked for permission from the church to establish their own church. Permission was granted and Scotts Creek Liberty Baptist was organized in a little log house in the Beta area of the county.

Around the same time, other black churches were being established. The River View Baptist Church was established in the River View section of Dillsboro and the Black Branch Methodist Church was organized at Hog Rock in the Little Savannah area. In 1892, at a little log house in Dix Gap, a Methodist church was established by former slaves and other former slaves from bordering states. The Methodist church moved to the Cullowhee area and located at the present day Roberson Dorm at Western Carolina University.

Rev. Charles Hemphill was one of the Hemphill brothers who pastored at Liberty Baptist Church in 1871 to 1875.

This is the shell of the African American Webster Baptist church taken in 1982. Shortly afterward, the church was destroyed by fire by persons unknown.

River View Baptist Church in the River View section of Dillsboro is now an empty shell. The brick veneered church closed its doors in the late 1960's because of migration. Smaller photo by Etheree Burkett Chancellor.

15

One of the three one-room black schools in Jackson County that was built around the 1880's. This school was located at the end of Dix Gap.

In 1866 Senator James R. Love, a native of Jackson County, proposed that school communities should never employ colored teachers to instruct white children. His motion was immediately amended to state that white teachers couldn't teach colored students. Thus, with the idea that the two races could not learn in the same environment, separate schools were instituted.

In 1869 in Jackson County, there were 90 African American children who were of school age. The Biennial Report of the Superintendent of Public Instruction began to report on African American schools for the county in 1882. Three African American public schools served the county with the school term lasting about 15 weeks. Total enrollment was 83 black children. These schools were probably located in Beta, Webster and East La Porte where the majority of African Americans lived.

On October 7, 1899 Cornelius Knox, Joseph Babb and W. C. Whittenberg purchased a half acre on the banks of Scotts Creek near the present day Liberty Baptist Church for a future school site.

16

1889—Miss Mattie J. Davis is one the school teachers who taught in one-room schools in the County. She taught at Webster's African American school. She also taught in the consolidated African American school.

The Sylva Tannery which was located in the Tannery Flats around the railroad track.

Some of the African Americans who worked at the Sylva Tannery were John Austin, Bob Bryson, Lee Howell, Clarence Love, Joe Love, Lester McDonald, Tom Pickens, Homer Whittenburg, McKinley Whittenburg, Joe Wilson, Grant Wilson and Josh Worley.

By the 20th century, the population of African Americans in the county reached almost 400. About 3% were miners. With Harris Enterprises and the opening of the Cullowhee Normal School, African Americans began to migrate to the center of the county.

White local men, David Hall and E. L. McKee, partnered with Harris in opening the tannery in East Sylva; hiring both black and white workers, they built company houses in the Tannery Flats. Little red company houses sat on the hillside, with white workers occupying those on the west end and African Americans on the upper end. African Americans from Hog Rock, Webster and Beta areas came to the Flats to obtain jobs in the tannery. These enterprising white businessmen also opened a general store, Sylva Supply, for the workers to purchase their supplies. Using store coupons they could obtain goods, but had to pay it back at payday.

The Sylva Supply was established by C. J. Harris in 1893 to supply his workers a store to obtain their needs. This photo was taken in 1981.

19

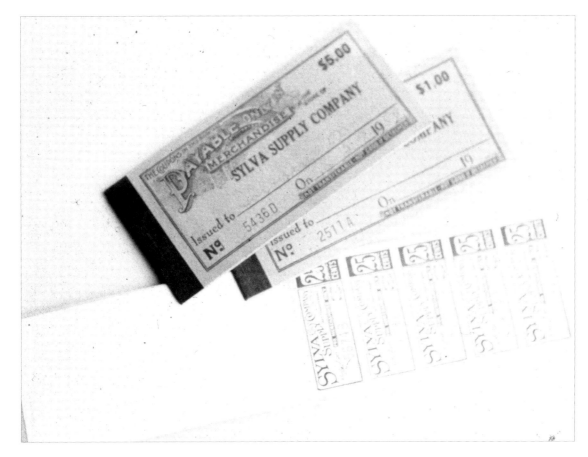

These coupon books were given to workers so that they could pay for their supplies. The worker had the money deducted from his weekly pay.

Others in the East Le Porte area moved to Cullowhee Valley to get jobs in the mines in Long Branch and at Cullowhee Normal School. As the decades went by, the Cullowhee Normal School hired African Americans as janitors, maids and cooks. Some were hired as teamsters to bring supplies from the depot in Sylva. Other African Americans hired themselves out as taxis to bring students and their luggage to the campus. The Normal School was fast becoming a boarding school and the African Americans provided their service.

These teamsters are coming from Sylva on the unpaved Cullowhee road.
They are hauling supplies for the Normal School from the train depot.
Among those teamsters was Mr. Robert Davis, who became head janitor at the school.

The main occupation of the African American male was that of a farmer or farm laborer. Others worked on the railroad or in the several mining operations in the county. At the turn of the century other skilled and unskilled workers were sawmill workers, day laborers, hotel porters, and carpenters.

One of these workers was Mr. Will Rogers. He was born in East La Porte and moved with his family to Monteith Gap on land his father Lemuel Rogers purchased. He grew up with several brothers and sisters. When World War I came and Governor T. W. Bickett called for volunteers for service, he was among the 15 African Americans from Cullowhee.

Private William Rogers — 1918

22

After World War I, Mr. Will Rogers returned to his home in Monteith Gap and married Stella Love. All of his siblings migrated to Washington D.C. Mr. Will became sole owner of his father's land. To feed his large family, he farmed his acreage of land and supplemented his income by working with Hester and McAfee Construction Company at Cullowhee Normal School. One of the white bricklayers taught Will how to do masonry work. Throughout his lifetime he used his skills as a mason to built chimneys and other structures in and around Western North Carolina.

Mr. Will was a family man and very religious. His father helped organize the Methodist Church in Dix Gap. Mr. Will worked diligently and faithfully in the church. He was there when the old church got its steeple and was a member of the removal team that reburied bodies from the old grave site at Roberson Dorm on WCU campus.

Will and Bolin Rogers — 1920

Hazel and Helen Rogers are twin daughters of Mr. Will and Stella Rogers. Their sister Louise was not quite a year older than the twins.

Hazel and Helen Rogers were born April 2, 1923. They grew up in Cullowhee and attended school at Sylva. They became members of Mt. Zion AME Zion Methodist Church of Cullowhee. They graduated from Central consolidated High in 1945. At one time, both worked at Western Carolina University. Helen, now deceased, married and moved to Marion, NC. Hazel retired from WCU. Louise also worked at WCU until she retired.

Mother and Son

George Power Casey and his mother Amanda Thomas Casey lived in Cullowhee.

Amanda Thomas was born in Oconaluftee area of Jackson County to Martha, enslaved to William Holland Thomas, the white chief of the Cherokees. She worked for Thomas until emancipation. On January 14, 1869, she legally married William Casey before Justice of the Peace C. C. Spake. Before this legal union, Amanda had a male child whom she named Mountville Sherman (1866). William Casey was listed as his father on his death certificate. Amanda and William (Bill) had five more children. They were James Henry (1869), Cordelia (1876), Delaware (1879), George Power (1882 and Charles Brane (1884).

Together the couple had purchased land in Cullowhee. In the late 1890's, when Bill left Amanda, she became the matriarch of the family. When she died, George inherited the land and raised his family there.

25

George's wife Sadie Hooper Casey and three of their children. On left is Estus, on the right is Henry and on her lap is Lee Roy — 1920.

Mr. Sherman Davis was the son of Silas Davis.

Mr. Sherman Davis met his wife, Josephine Moore, when he was one of her students at the one-room school in Cullowhee.

His first job was as a miner at the mica mine in Cullowhee. Later, he delivered milk for Sunny Brook Dairy (Pet). He left the dairy for another job when the Mead Corporation came to the county.

Some time later, Mr. Sherman opened a small grocery store in the Tannery Flats. Since all his children were grown, this enterprise kept his wife out of mischief.

Charlie Casey and a friend posing for the camera —1930's

Being alienated from the white society, African Americans found their own society within their churches and schools. A Methodist and a Baptist church were established in each community. The Black Branch Methodist Church at Hog Rock closed its doors as the African Americans migrated to Sylva to find employment. They established another Methodist church in the heart of the Tannery Flats. The church was built in 1914. By this time both Methodist churches were members of AME Zion. They became circuit churches with one pastor serving both churches. The itinerant pastor would hold services at the Mt. Zion Cullowhee Church on the first and third Sundays and Maize Chapel on the second and fourth Sundays.

of the bodies would occur. The task would be conducted under the direction of Rev. W. L. Lawhorn, the church pastor. There were 86 bodies removed and reburied, along with an amputated arm.

Mr. Will Rogers was the foreman of the reburying crew.

Mt. Zion AME (African Methodist Episcopal) Zion church in Cullowhee was built 1929 on the other side of the hill from WCTC.

While Black Branch members moved to Sylva, Mt. Zion found that they had to move again after migrating to the Cullowhee area. The Cullowhee Normal School had become Western Carolina Teachers' College. The African American church was situated on the hill near the college and WCTC needed the land for expansion. The college secured options from the African American church. On May 25, 1928 a report to the college board of trustees stated that the purchase of the property was in the process of been settled. The African American community thought that the college was going to plow up the graves, but they were reassured that the removal

These two unidentified ladies are dressed in the style of the era—1920's

In the early 1900's, the African American separate one-room schools were becoming extinct. In 1919 the one-room schools in Webster and Sylva had consolidated. The Cullowhee School Committee refused to send their children to the consolidated school. They wanted to maintain their own community school. However, their one-room school on College Hill was in much need of repair. The Cullowhee African Americans wanted to build a new school beside Mt. Carmel Baptist Church in Monteith Gap. Some lumber was already there to begin the project.

The school was never built, as the Jackson County system convinced them that consolidation would provide more for the African American students. Not only that, the county built a new African American school on Scotts Creek just adjacent to Liberty Baptist Church.

Central Consolidated School was built in 1924 for the African American children in the county. Busing for the African American students had begun. In the beginning the school was called Colored Consolidated School and was considered a distinct credit to the county. The Julius Rosenwald Fund contributed $1,450 dollars to the school's construction.

From the teachers of the one-room schools in the county, Jackson County's school board selected Rev. John H. Davis as the principal of the consolidated school, although his wife Carrie had been the principal at River View and Webster schools.

Rev. John H. Davis—first principal of Central Consolidated School—was from Reidsville, NC. He was the brother of Mattie J. Davis.

Rev. and Mrs. John H. Davis and Family—1920
John H. Davis, shown here with his family in Webster, oversaw the education of Jackson County's African American students for 22 years, from 1919 until his retirement in 1942.

CHAPTER 3 — DURING AND AFTER WORLD WAR I & II (1930-1949)

In the 1930's the nation experienced a depression. Jackson County felt it. However, African American communities continued to try to improve their lot. After World War I there was little migration. Most of the residents were farmers and they continued to work the land. Others found work in the white educational institution as cooks, housekeepers and janitors. Some obtained jobs with the CCC and other government jobs. With the consolidation of the African American schools and improved road system in the county, the African American communities were slowly becoming one. The school united them, as did the church.

With the itinerant pastors, most churches didn't have services on the fifth Sundays. Therefore, the African Americans organized a fifth Sunday meeting with all the churches, both Baptist and Methodist to come together under one roof. With about five fifth Sundays in a year, each church had a chance to hold the meeting. There was Sunday school, morning service, eating on the ground, afternoon service and night service. All the monies raised would go to the host churches.

It was during 1940's that all schools were required to provide a diploma when the students completed the twelfth grade. Central Consolidated only went to the tenth grade. A lot of the students went to other schools in the Western North Carolina area to complete their education so that they could go on to college.

Rev. Silas Rogers, brother of Will Rogers, became a minister and moved to Johnson City, TN. He was one of the many African Americans who migrated to the "city."

John Johnson and Henry Casey
relaxing after work. 1936

*Estus Casey and his future wife
DeRosette Horne are at his father
George Casey's home in Cullowhee. 1934*

Laura Una is working at the Carolina Hotel in Sylva on Main Street—1940's

Mrs. Katherine Wells and Mrs. Susie Bryson were employed by Western Carolina Teachers College at Cullowhee.

Clarissa Coward and Melvine Chavis are two matriarchs in the African American community of Cullowhee—1948

Clarissa and Melvine were affectionately called "Aunt" by the African American children. Aunt Clarissy had learned the art of magical healing and practiced it throughout the community. She could take a sty out of the eye of an individual using one of her many healing remedies.

Aunt Mel was a midwife. She helped bring a lot of babies into the world. She assisted my mother DeRosette with the birth of most of her middle children, including me. She lived just above us and was on hand for the birth of Lorinda, Brenda, myself and twin brothers Victor and Floretta.

Charlie Bryson, who went up North to find work, is the husband of Susie Bryson.

Mr. Charlie Bryson worked in the Tannery for thirty years before it closed. However, there was no retirement plan. In the 1940's when the auto business was booming, he went to Detroit and obtained a job on the assembly line at General Motors to help support his family. He left his family in Sylva. He did seasonal work and returned home for the winter to be with his family.

The African American population was relatively small compared to the white population in Jackson County. It was difficult to start a business and maintain it without the white population supporting it. In the early 1900's, Rev. J. C. McKinney, minister of Maize Chapel AME Zion church in the Tannery Flats, opened a laundry business on the back street of Sylva. He employed some members of his church to work. The laundry closed because of financial difficulties. Another major factor was that Rev. McKinney was reassigned to another church.

Another laundry was opened the late 1930's. Mr. Odell Bryson operated a laundry from his home in the Tannery Flats. His customers were both whites and African Americans. He was able to maintain this business until the late 1940's.

Mr. Sherman Davis's grocery store was another African American enterprise that opened in the Flats. He opened it in the early 1940's. Davis Grocery was in operation until Mr. Davis became ill in the 1970s.

Davis Grocery, located in the middle of the Tannery Flats, was established in the early 1940's. This picture was taken in 1982. The building was torn down in 2006.

Webster Baptist Church was perhaps the birthplace of the ***Feast in the Wilderness.*** Traditionally it was a Sunday when white politicians came to the African American churches to state their positions for the upcoming election. With backing of the other African American churches in the county the *Feast in the Wilderness* became a regular event every fifth Sunday.

*

This is River View Baptist Church where Mr. Jim Wells was a member. He headed the Feast in the Wilderness. Below is part of the minutes of the Feast held at River View on July 30, 1939.

The Minutes for R. V. B. Church

July 30-1939. Sunday Evening

The Great Feast in the Wilderness.
ed to represent with $1.00.

Webster Church Rep. $1.00
River view Church $1.00
Liberty Church $1.00

C. M. E. Zion Church ... $1.00
Collection for the day was. $11.18. one dollar to pay
leaving amount $ $10.18.

Rev. and Mrs. Joe H. Smith — 1971

Rev. Joseph Henry Smith, a native son, became pastor of Scotts Creek Liberty Baptist Church in 1928. Through his leadership the church grew. On the tiny plank structure, they built an addition to accommodate the growing congregation. A new church was built in 1942.

Joseph Henry Smith was born on December 26, 1903. His mother was Bessie Marjorie Love Smith. He was reared by an extended family of aunts, uncles and a grandfather. His grandfather Joseph Smith told Rev. Smith about being a slave. Being in a religious family, he listened as his grandfather sang hymns.

As a young boy, he went to the one-room school on Scotts Creek about a mile from downtown Sylva. He found it difficult to attend school. After learning the basics, he went to live with Rev. Anderson Wilson. He attended Calvary Presbyterian High in Asheville and learned carpentry.

Along with his secular education, he studied the Bible under Rev. Wilson's guidance. This was Smith's apprenticeship to the ministry. For eight years, he learned from his mentor the ways of the Bible. Around the Rev. Wilson's table there were always conversations about the Holy Scripture. At seventeen, Joseph Henry Smith was ordained by the church in Brevard and accepted his first pastorship in Yancey County in 1920. In 1928 he became not only the pastor at Liberty, but also at Mt. Olive Baptist in Mars Hill.

It was at Mars Hill he met his wife Syrilda Hampton. He baptized her and a romance blossomed. They were married November 17, 1932. They settled down in Sylva where they raised their daughter Marjorie.

At one time, Rev. Smith was pastoring four churches. Besides Liberty and Mt. Olive, he had Mt. Olive of Waynesville and Mt. Nebo of Lake Lure.

*It is a Sunday afternoon and the church members of Liberty Baptist have gathered at the
creek bank for a baptism. In the background on the left is Liberty Baptist Church
and on the right is Central Consolidated School —1940*

This picture was taken on a summer afternoon at Liberty Baptist Church's Vacation Bible School (VBS). This building was erected in 1942 after Rev. Smith saw that the old plank building was falling apart. On the 4th Sunday of May, they marched into this new rock veneer building.

Vacation Bible School at Liberty Baptist was an annual event for all the black children in the county.

In the late 1940's VBS's were held at Mt. Zion in Cullowhee as well as Liberty Baptist. Mt. Zion had assistance from white Cullowhee Methodist Church.

By the early 1950's Mt. Zion had ceased to hold VBS. On the other hand, Liberty Baptist continued. Being the largest African American church in the county and having a pastor who lived in the community, all the African American children were invited to attend. Rev. Smith would truck African American children from outlying communities of Cullowhee and Dillsboro in his red pickup truck.

Today Liberty continues to reach out into other communities to attend their VBS.

Minnie Casey holding her step-grandson, Joseph and Joseph's father Lee Roy Casey posed for this photo after church service at Mt. Zion AME Zion Church at Cullowhee —1936.

Three generations—"Sis" McDowell holding her son Joe Louis with her mother, Mrs. Gertrude McDowell — 1936

45

Sherman (Buddy) Alston, son of Mr. and Mrs. John Alston enlisted in the army and fought in World War II in France. His commanding officer wrote his mother, fondly known as "Aunt Della," to comment on his bravery in action.

Della Casey Alston, mother of Sherman Alston, relaxing in her backyard.

1920-30's Gallery

Hattie Davis

Mr. Thad Allen

*Maxine Whittenberg
and Aunt Dorothy Allen*

Cary May Casey Gray
as she aged from a girl
in the early 1900's to
the "Roaring 20's" to a
mature woman in the
1930's

48

Children of the Allen Sisters:
Jimbo Allen
Bobby Allen
Billy Casey

Mr. McKinley Whittenberg
Mr. Jay Durham

Flood of 1940

This is the house of Mr. and Mrs. Robert Davis which was located on the Tuckasegee river on the lower river road (Casey Road) in Cullowhee. Mrs. Davis loved her home so much that she had to be bodily removed from the flooding river. After the flood, the Davis family relocated; however, this time they built on a hillside.

FACULTY MEMBERS OF CENTRAL CONSOLIDATED SCHOOL
1940-1941

Rev. John H. Davis, principal; Marion Howell, Ralph Davis, Birdell Davis, and Frank Davis are the faculty members of Central Consolidated School. In the background is the school bus that picked up African American children from the areas of Cullowhee, Dillsboro, and Sylva.

This faculty is fondly called "The Davis Connection." Rev. John H. Davis is Ralph Davis' father. Birdell Davis is Rev Davis' niece and Frank Davis is not related. In the African American schools in Jackson County, the African American students affectively called the male teachers professors. However, instead of saying "professor," they were called "'Fessor."

The dilemma for the faculty was that all the male teachers had the same last name. To distinguish between the three, Ralph and Frank were called by their first names, and the principal was "'Fessor" Davis. In other words, Ralph was called "'Fessor" Ralph and Frank was called "'Fessor" Frank. Until their deaths, both men were addressed this way.

Central Consolidated School's tenth grade graduation class of about 1939.

John Wade Sr.

John Wade Sr. became principal of Central Consolidated School in 1942. He was from Bluefield, West Virginia. When he was hired, he was teaching in Murphy, North Carolina. He married a local girl, Mae Studderth. The couple moved to Sylva and had three children.

Tenth Grade Graduation Class of 1942

Ralph H. Davis became a member of CHS faculty in 1935. He taught under his father John H. Davis for 13 years. He left and went to teach and coach at Reynolds High School in Canton. —1944.

'Fessor Davis the homeroom teacher of this 1940 graduating class of CHS poses with his students. The mascots are Shirley Davis, Davis' daughter and Claude Wells, son of Mr. and Mrs. Jim Wells. On the far right is Lyndon Casey, next to him is Helen Rogers and her twin sister, Hazel is the fourth one on from the right. Between the Rogers twins is Lula Mae Murray (Sanders).

Ruth Casey

Ruth, daughter of Charlie and Hattie Casey, was educated in the African American school system in Jackson County. She went to Allen Home in Asheville to complete her high school education. Afterward she attended a Normal School down east where she obtained her teaching license. She then came back home to teach at Central Consolidated School. She taught there for three years from 1941 to 1944.

Mrs. Jennie Nance Carter from Connecticut was the primary teacher from 1944 to 1951. She was one of the first teachers to have an "A" Certificate.

Two school girls—Virginia Bennett and Ann Rogers—from Cullowhee were bussed to Central Consolidated School in Sylva.

The picture above depicts a baseball team of the late 1940's. It appears to be a school team, perhaps one of the schools where African Americans sent their sons to finish their education.

Baseball was a favorite sport for the African Americans in Jackson County. As far back as the early 1900's, it was their summertime pastime. When the Tannery was built, a baseball field was laid adjacent to it. Many African American workers played ball there. Wilsy Dorsey was considered one the best players in the county.

When the African American schools consolidated, a ball field was built adjacent to it. The

56

school children played ball there during recess. The two large communities of African Americans formed a baseball team. Cullowhee's team was the Slow-Sluggers and Sylva was the Red Sox.

These ball teams became rivals and played some tight games since each team wanted to be considered Jackson County's best. They would play each other on the 4th of July and the white fans would join in cheering for their community team.

The two ball teams finally combined their efforts and became one team. This was because of the outward migration of African Americans during the 1940's and 1950's. They chose to adopt the name Red Sox.

Boys Basketball teams in the late 1930's or early 1940'S

Top: Girls from Jackson County are pictured above at Allen Home, Asheville, NC.

Inset: Girls representing the Jackson County's basketball team.

Central Consolidated High boys' basketball team is playing an all-white city team at the Whittier Gym. CHS played these city teams to fill in the schedule. The African American players from left to right are James Streater, Dan Bryson, Charles Pickens and Herbert Dean Streater—1952

Central Consolidated High School girls' basketball team is playing an all-white city team at Whittier Gym. CHS played city teams to fill in the schedule. The African American players from left to right are Betty Jo Worley, Dorothy Worley and Dorothy Howell.

CHAPTER 4 — THE ONSET OF CHANGE (1950-1965)

The 1950's came on the scene and the African Americans in Jackson County continued to have the Feast in the Wilderness on the fifth Sundays. However, members of the Liberty Baptist had pulled out of the organization and formed their own Fifth Sunday Meeting among the three churches Rev Smith pastored as well as New Hope Baptist Church of Knoxville.

The African Americans now began to stand up openly for their rights through the courts. A landmark decision came with the case of Brown vs. Topeka—which stated that the educational system across the country was not equal and desegregation had to be done "with all deliberate speed."

And yet as the much publicized Civil Rights Movement began and Jackson County and the world watched on television, the local African Americans did nothing. They continued to bond their communities through Boy Scouts, womens clubs, and other organizations that eclipsed religious denominations. Everything remained the status quo.

The African American population in Jackson County remained calm about the Civil Rights Movement situation and did nothing. During this time it was plain to see that the white population admired the African American athletic abilities and desired to have them on their high school sports teams.

Neither side, black or white, made a move to change the county. When John F. Kennedy became president and was assassinated, the status quo remained.

But, now, in county sports, African American boys were encouraged to participate. Times were changing. It wasn't until 1964 that partial integration occurred. The curtain was beginning to be torn down.

Bussing continued in Jackson County for the African American students as Jackson County School Bus #18 delivered them to and from school. It traveled to Cullowhee, Dillsboro and Sylva.

61

Minnie & Lyndon Casey

Mr. Homer Rogers who lived on Long Branch in Cullowhee made friends in both worlds.

Romaine Casey, Henry Casey's daughter-in-law, holding Freddie Casey. Standing in front is Henry's nephew, Robert Lynn Mebane.

Henry Casey with his family and friends are on an outing. From left to right is Henry, nephew Robert Lynn Mebane on his shoulder, his wife Jessie Casey, a friend Mrs. Annie Dorsey, and sister-in-law Margie Casey—1951

The African Americans in Jackson County have come a long way. The journey has been hard, but prosperous. Now, no longer relying on the farm, they have made their way to the industrial world.

However, it is reassuring that George Estus Casey loved to farm, and loved his animals—1933. (author's father)

Clifford Casey, shown here in the inset and shoeing, learned the art of being a Farrier from his father Mr. George Casey who once managed a black-smith shop in Cullowhee.

Mr. Charles Walton was a janitor at Jackson School in 1957. He was a pianist at Liberty Baptist Church.

Mr. Dave Rogers was born and raised in Jackson County, but moved away. He would always visit his family and relatives in the summertime—1950

In the center is Jesse Howell, Jr. in the army uniform and his brother and friend from left to right Ray Worley and Charles Bryson. Howell served in the Korean War—1952

Mrs. Essie Hampton Casey was the mother of Mrs. Syrilda Smith. She married George Casey in 1945. George's children affectively called her Mama Essie. This was George's third wife—1958

Webster Baptist Church, with its beauty still sensed in this photo, was the scene of many Feasts in the Wilderness.

Maize Chapel AME Zion Church

The circuit churches of Mt. Zion of Cullowhee and Maize Chapel of Sylva were part of the *Feast in the Wilderness.* The last evidence of the feast came at Maize Chapel AME Zion Methodist Church on October 31, 1965. Maize Chapel was designed by Mr. Dallas Grey, who was a member of the church as well as a carpenter. Mr. Will Rogers stated that he did all the masonry work.

A Scene from the "Feast in the Wilderness"

Here, Mt. Zion of Cullowhee is hosting the *Feast in the Wilderness.* Pictured above from left to right are Mrs. Beulah Lackey, Miss Mary Wells, Mrs. Katherine Wells, Mrs. Mellie Chavis, Mrs. Rosie Love and Mrs. Hattie Lackey. Mrs. Katherine Wells and her daughter Mary, were members of River View Baptist, Mrs. Beulah Lackey and sister-in-law Mrs. Hattie Lackey were members of Mt. Zion—1951

Mrs. Mary Lowery seen here seated in her
living room was a member of Mt. Zion AME
Zion Church in Cullowhee—1951

Rev. Richard Terry, shown here on the left, was the pastor of the Methodist circuit churches in Cullowhee and Sylva. He and his family lived in the Sylva Tannery Flats area in a house provided by both churches.

Mrs. Fredericka Love was one of the teachers in the one-room schools in the Beta/Scotts Creek areas. She belonged to Liberty Baptist Church and was a very active member.

It was traditionally stated that she was a staunch Baptist and tried to prevent members from attending other dominations.

On January 10, 1958, shortly after the funeral service of Bessie Worley, the Scotts Liberty Baptist Church caught fire from the faulty furnace. By the time the voluntary fire department arrived the building was fully engulfed in flames.

Liberty not only lost its church, but some of their written history went up in smoke. Rev. Smith had stored a lot of the church documents in the belfry.

Determined to rebuild, they had a period of prayer and reflection. After that they gathered at the pastor's home and pledged to support the program. With the help of the African American and white communities, the church was rebuilt by December 1959 at a cost of about $16,000 dollars.

This is the Scotts Creek Liberty Baptist Senior Choir. They are among the many church auxiliaries who helped rebuild the church with their donations and fund raisers.

The author's great uncle & aunt,
Charlie & Hattie Casey

*Charlie & Hatti's nephew
Leroy Casey — about the 1930's*

Three Sisters

Mrs. Marion Alston, Mrs. Otylia Studderth and Mrs. Carrie Howell Scruggs. These sisters are the daughters of Mr. and Mrs. John Alston.

Mr. Lawrence Allen (Pappa)
with grandson Joe Gibson

Catherine Blakely

*Robby and Tammy Bryson,
daughers of Mr. and Mrs. John
Robert Bryson.*

*Leon, James, and Rudy
McDonald*

76

Interdenominational learning session in the 1950's at Liberity Baptish Church

Junior Choir at Liberty Baptist Church —1950's (under the direction of Miss Edith Howell)
Front Row: Brenda Bryson, Trudy Whittenberg, Beverley Wade.
Back Row: Pauline Allen and Marquinta Wade

In the 1950's things began to change once more for the African American school. Before the decade ended a new school had been erected. Under the leadership of 'Fessor Wade, the school hired "A" certificate teachers and those who didn't meet the standards were fired.

Basketball players honored the school by winning the conference with a 21-1 record for the 1953-54 seasons. With the help of their white friends, a football program was initiated. Clarence Love, son of Mrs. Fredericka Love was hired as a science teacher in the high school program. This program lasted for two years before it ended for lack of participants. Macon and Swain Counties sent their African American high school students to Jackson County because of the small numbers in their segregated school systems. With the increase of the male population in the high school and the lack of academic requirements, Central Consolidated High School ran a football program. When Macon County

established Chapel High, an African American school, the football program was dropped in Jackson County for lack of players.

Between 1949 and 1954, the African American community repeatedly requested a new building from the Board of Education, but the issue was always tabled. Finally, Raleigh sent a committee to conduct a survey of African American students in the three counties. The committee recommended building a high school in the African American community of Sylva to serve Macon and Swain students also. The three counties were to share the cost.

However, when Macon County saw that they would have to pay about 35% of the cost, their Board of Education felt it would be more feasible that the money be used to extend their African American elementary school. Thus Macon County African American high school students no longer came to Jackson County. When Brown vs. Topeka was passed in 1954, the bid for the African

American school project was collected. Plans were halted, but they opened again in 1955 and the plans were approved. The African American representatives were Mr. Will Rogers, Mr. Charlie Casey, Mr. M. Curry, Rev. Smith and 'Fessor Wade, who assured the Board that "all blacks in Jackson wanted the continuation of a segregated school system' and the building of a new school was imperative.

Mrs. Margaret Sue Streater Miller was hired in 1951 as teacher for the 1st through 4th grades. The classroom was huge and crowded. Teaching four grade levels was challenging.

Mrs. Miller taught at Central Consolidated and Jackson School until the African American school closed in 1965. She was not only a classroom teacher, but also the girls' basketball coach.

This is the 1952 football team for Central Consolidated High. The head coach on the left is Clarence Love and the assistant coach is John W. Wade.

The 1953-54 CHS Boys Basketball Team.

The first string of CHS White Phantoms are, from left to right, Frank Davis, assistant coach; Charles Dorsey, Charles Norman, James Streater, Daniel Bryson, Herbert Dean Streater, and Clarence Love, head coach.

This basketball team of CHS lost only one game for the season and won the conference championship at Reynolds High in Canton. Playing city teams, white or black, and other African American schools in Western North Carolina, the White Phantom racked up a 21-1 record. In 2000, the Jackson County Athletic Hall of Fame honored them at their annual banquet.

In September of 1956 the new African American school opened its doors to the students. The school had inside plumbing and a central heating system. The building was large, with enough room for primary and elementary areas. On each side of the long narrow corridor were two huge classrooms. Two were for the high school students and other two for the elementary students.

Housed in one room were the first to fourth graders, and the other room held fifth to eighth graders. In the high school area the first room was homeroom to the freshmen and sophomores, while the other room was homeroom to the juniors and seniors.

With these multiple grade levels housed all together, they held classes together. There was no room for a library, but shelves in the back of the underclassmen classroom sufficed. The gym, only large enough for a regulation court, had little room for an audience to sit around the sides.

However, most importantly, it was a brand new school.

ALMA MATER
Song

At the foot of Balsm Mountain
on the rollin green

Stands our noble Alma Mato
like a light house beam.

Chorus

CENTRAL CENTRAL how we love you
with your black and white

HAIL to thee our Alma Mato
Hail to CENTRAL HIGH.

Jackson School—the new school for the Africa American community
which delayed integration for nine years.

In the center is Principal 'Fessor
John W. Wade. On the left is
Annie Ruth Howell and on the
right is Walter Wells—1956.

The 1956-1957 Jackson High basketball teams.
From left are Alberta Young, Mary Wells, Linda Bryson, Margaret Conley, Sybil Davis,
Jacqueline Bryson, Permelia Casey, Annie Ruth Howell, Yvonne Bryson, Alice Tate
and Geraldyne Casey.

The 1956-1957 Jackson High boys' basketball team. Kneeling from left to right are Charles Jones, Homer Whittenberg, Johnnie Wade, Fred Howell. Standing from left to right are Walter Wells, Harry Howell, Coach John W. Wade, Nathanael Coleman and Claude Young.

'Fessor Frank K. Davis became principal of Jackson School in 1957. He had taught at the African American school since 1940. His mother Josephine Moore Davis was a teacher at the one-room school in Cullowhee.

Each year, the senior class would donate an item to the Jackson School. This flag pole base was donated by the class of 1961. Today this building houses the Jackson County Board of Education. The flag pole is still there.

John Robert Bryson relaxing on break at work in the WCU Cafeteria.

Sherman Davis and Mamie Curry dressed to go out on the town.

List of Photos

It is now the 21st century and Jackson County has taken on a new face, not only in the white community, but also in the African American community. Many original African Americans who settled here after the Civil War have migrated to the North and the West of these United States. Some still call Jackson County home while others vow never to come home again.

Dreams of those who came before, like streaks of lightning, have finally come alive across the county. The African Americans in Jackson have now stepped up to the plate and are moving not only in social interaction with the establishment, but also within the political arena. It happened this way.

After the integration of the schools, African American student-athletes continued to display their talents on the athletic field as well as in the classroom. One of the first excellent athletes to be recognized was Tommy Love who dominated the football field when playing for Sylva-Webster. College scouts from across the country came to see him and offered him full four-year scholarships to Division I colleges. After graduation, he chose Michigan State. During his sophomore year, he died tragically of a heart attack.

Tommy was among the group of students who were the first to integrate the all-white schools in the county. The other students who enrolled at Sylva-Webster High School were Eugene Austin, LeRoy Jackson, and Mary Francis Jackson. Virginia Hampton and Johnny Bryson enrolled in the Camp Lab School in Cullowhee.

This was only the beginning.

The young black athletes were able to excel in the "big" arena of the integrated schools. The Streater children whose father was James Streater made their mark in football, basketball and baseball.

Western Carolina University integrated its campus and the local African Americans had a chance to obtain a college education without leaving home. Floretta Casey was one of the first to earn her bachelor's degree and elementary school teacher's certification. Recently she retired from the Greenville City Schools system.

African Americans began to sit on important committees in the county. They earned teaching positions in the county.

When total integration first came, the two local teachers, Mr. Frank K. Davis and Mrs. Miller had to find jobs. Mrs. Miller was hired at Camp Lab, but Mr. Davis had to go to Macon County, where he obtained a job at LBJ Job Corps near Franklin. It has proved to be an uphill battle for an African American to secure a teaching job in the county.

A few have succeeded. In 1976, I was hired at Log Cabin Elementary School and moved to Smokey Mountain Elementary when Qualla and Log Cabin consolidated in 1980. I enjoyed 28 years of service. Mary Sue Casey came home to teach at Smoky Mountain High after beginning her teaching in Monroe, NC. Currently, other African Americans teach in the the county school system.

In the law enforcing service, Danny Allen became the first African American policeman in the town of Sylva. He was elected town commissioner and ran for mayor.

Donnie Allen became the first African American deputy sheriff. Lyndon Casey, Jr. went to Highway Patrolman School and is now stationed in Asheville.

More and more opportunities are within the grasp of the African American citizens who now call Jackson County home. It's not easy, for there is still prejudice within the county. One of the shining beams of light for the African American community is called "Bridges to Community," encouraged by Sylva Mayor Brenda Oliver. Mary Sue Casey is president of the group.

Leroy Jackson & Jackie Turner—first cousins; grandsons of Mrs. Grace Bryson.

Mrs. Grace, mother of 17 children, is shown below with more of her grandchildren.

Acknowledgements

First, I would like to express my sincere thanks to Ray Menze, president of the Jackson County Arts Council and the entire membership of the Jackson County Arts Council for sponsoring this historical picture of the African Americans in Jackson County, North Carolina.

Along with the Arts Council, I appreciate the work of the Ammons sisters and their non-profit heritage organization, Catch the Spirit of Appalachia, for assisting me in this publication. Included in this note of thanks is also the help received from the North Carolina Community Foundation, who also helped to fund the book.

I would be amiss if I did not thank Livingston Photo for their help in developing my slides into manageable photographs. And I am most grateful for the assistance of the Sandbox at Western Carolina University. Sharon Ferguson, a friend and computer wizard, I wish to thank for recovering and burning the manuscript text to a CD. Without her patience and understanding, my manuscript would be lost. I thank Marie Cochran for her bubbling energy and advice that this book should be my own. I thank you.

Now, I must thank the African American community for providing me with family pictures of their ancestors. Collecting their photographs has been a long and tedious journey. Mostly, I must acknowledge my family and the Casey Family Reunion for their support. I am most grateful to all those who have encouraged me without even knowing that you did. I thank you, I thank you.

Last, but not least, I am most grateful to my daughter Tina, who endured all my frustrations. I love you dearly and I thank you from the bottom of my heart.

To all of you...God Bless.

—*Victoria A. Casey McDonald*

This is the new generation that has embarked on the journey of becoming an important part of the establishment. Clockwise from the right are Mary Sue Casey, Audrey Casey, Mamie Sue Love and Lyndon Casey, Jr. In the background are Mrs. Dorothy Love, Mamie Sue's mother, Dorothy Worley, the Casey children's aunt and Minnie Casey, the Casey children's mother.

Timeline of the African American Experience in Jackson Conty
1800 — 1965

1800's   Daniel Bryson came across Balsam with 140 slaves and settled in the Beta area.

1820-25   Joshua Hall purchased Aunt Ede and brothers, Sid and Icem from near Petersburg, Virginia. Around the same time period William Holland Thomas purchased Martha, my great-great grandmother from Virginia.

1830-50   William Holland Thomas sold and traded slaves.

1850   Approximately 23 slave owners and 185 slaves were listed in the census records in the area that was to become Jackson County. Only three owned more than ten slaves.

1851   Jackson County was formed from Macon and Haywood Counties.

1860   46 slaveholders owned 226 slaves. Seven owned more than ten slaves.

1860-1865 Civil War.

     Cudge, a slave of W.H. Thomas served his master as a body servant during the war.

1865   Emancipation.

1866-1869 Slaves who "jumped the broom" legalized their marriages.

1868   Mining company opened in the county with black and white workers.

1870   Jackson County showed an influx of former slaves from bordering states (Georgia, South Carolina) into the county. There were 33 black farmers listed and 66 black farm laborers in the county's census. The black population was 266.

1879-1871 Black churches began to be established in the county. Mr. Jim Wells traditionally stated that the black Webster Baptist Church was the first black church in the county.

1871   In May, former slaves Moses Bryson, Sip Bryson, Ella Bryson, Betsy Bryson, Lucinda Love, Sylvia Bryson, Rena Bryson, Abby Bryson, Elizabeth Bryson and Dorcus Love received permission from Scotts Creek Baptist Church to establish their own church; thus, Scotts Creek Liberty Baptist Church was born.

1890-1900 The River View Baptist Church was established in Dillsboro. In Hog Rock, a Methodist Church was established on Black Branch. Allen McDowell and his wife Rachel were members.

1892   A little log house in Dix Gap provided a location for the next Methodist Church. It was organized by Henry and Sarah Gaither, Gabriel and Laura Hooper, Lewis Rogers, Wilburn and Julie McDonald, William and Mellie Hooper and Wilson and Mary Lowery. Later they moved the church to Cullowhee, locating it at present day Roberson Dorm on the WCU campus.

1888   Colonel C.J. Harris, a Republican from Connecticut, built an industrial empire in the county. He hired black and white workers in his mining and tanning industries in the Sylva and Dillsboro areas.

1889   Robert Lee Madison established the Cullowhee Normal School (Western Carolina University) and black people found employment there.

1900   The African American population was almost at 400. 20 African Americans were miners. African Americans began to migrate into the center of the county.

1900   Liberty Baptist Church moved from the little log house to worship in the school.

1901   With local businessmen and former slave holders, David Hall and E.L. McKee, Harris opened a tannery in East Sylva.

1903   On December 8th, Peter Bryson, William Whitmire and Rev. J. S. Ritchie of Liberty Baptist purchased one-half acre of land adjoining the school property for the church.

1908-1910   Henry Gaither, George Love, Wilburn McDonald, Gab and Laura Hooper organized Mt. Carmel Baptist Church in Monteith Gap in Cullowhee.

1914   Methodist Church in Sylva was established when most of the members of the Black Branch Methodist Church (like Allen & Rachel McDowell) moved to Sylva to find jobs.

1919   Dillsboro and Sylva black schools consolidated to Sylva. A division of Negro Education was established in Raleigh in the office of the Superintendent of Public Instruction. Cullowhee Colored School Committee refused to consolidate.

1924   A new consolidated school was built in Sylva and all African American children were bussed there. Rev. John Davis became principal.

1929	Mt. Zion AME Zion Church moved. They moved 86 graves and an amputated arm.
1939	The first evidence of the Feast in the Wilderness on July 30 at River View Baptist Church.
1940	Liberty Baptist razed the old building and began working on a new structure.
1941-42	John Davis retired as principal at Central Consolidated School. John W. Wade, Sr. of Bluefield, West Virginia was hired.
1942	On the 4th Sunday in May, Liberty Baptist marched into the new building of rock veneer.
1945	Swain & Macon Counties eighth grade--high school black students were bused to Sylva.
1948	North Carolina Assembly required that all high schools be four years. Central Consolidated complied.
1954	Supreme Court decision that separate but equal wasn't equal and Macon County established their own black high school.
1955	The County School Board approved a new school plan. Black representatives were Will Rogers, Charlie Casey, M. Curry, Rev. J.H. Smith and John W. Wade.
1956	A new brick structure for the black students.
1957	John W. Wade departed and Frank K. Davis became principal.
1958	On January 10th, Liberty Baptist was destroyed by fire.
1959	On the last Sunday in December services were held in the new building.
1964	Partial integration. On August 21st, Leroy Jackson, Mary Jackson, Tommy Love, Eugene Austin, Johnny Bryson and Virginia Hampton went to their district white schools.
1965	May 27th--last commencement program at the black school. Complete integration for the next school year.

Victoria A. Casey McDonald is an ordained minister with God's Holy Tabernacle. She is the daughter of the late Mr. and Mrs. Estus Casey of Cullowhee, North Carolina. Educated in the segregated schools of Jackson County, she finished high school at Jackson High in 1961. Immediately after high school, Victoria enrolled and finished the Famous Artists Correspondence School and Famous Writers Correspondence School courses.

While enrolled in the correspondence school, she worked as a domestic servant. Shortly afterward, she obtained a job as a telephone operator at the local telephone company.

In her late twenties, Victoria began her college education at Western Carolina University and received her BA degree in History in 1973. Five years later, through the 11th Cycle of Teacher Corps at WCU, she obtained her teaching degree and MA in Education. After beginning her teaching career at Log Cabin School, she moved to Smokey Mountain Elementary when Log Cabin and Qualla Elementary consolidated. After 28 years of teaching and coaching on the elementary level, Rev. Casey McDonald retired. She came out of retirement and taught at Smoky Mountain High for a year and a half.

On a personal level, Rev. Casey McDonald was married to the late James E. McDonald, Sr. and they are the parents of a daughter, Tina. Her son, Creighton Casey is deceased. She enjoys bowling, writing, and researching local black history which includes genealogical history of her family.

A published writer of many poems speaking of her beliefs, Victoria was also the editor of The Nomad Literary Magazine while going to WCU.

Rev. Casey McDonald is vice-president of the Jackson County Arts Council and secretary of Bridges to Community. ∎